You Might Be A Preacher If...
Volume 2

A laugh-a-page look at the life of a pastor.

by Stan Toler
and
Mark Toler-Hollingsworth

Albury Publishing
P.O. Box 470406
Tulsa, Oklahoma 74147

You Might Be A Preacher If... Volume 2
ISBN 1-57778-030-2
Copyright © 1997 by Stan Toler & Mark Toler-Hollingsworth
P.O. Box 950
Bethany, Oklahoma 73008

Illustrated by Cory Edwards

Published by ALBURY PUBLISHING
P.O. Box 470406
Tulsa, Oklahoma 74147

Printed in the United States of America. All rights reserved under International Copyright Law. Contents and/or cover may not be reproduced in whole or in part in any form without the express written consent of the Publisher.

Dedication

To our church families —— Edmond First Church of the Nazarene, Edmond, Oklahoma (Pastor Mark) and Trinity Church of the Nazarene, Oklahoma City, Oklahoma (Pastor Stan).

Thanks for the love and laughter we experience each Sunday!

Special Thanks

To Jeannie Black and to the Albury Publishing team.

Introduction

It is with great joy that we present Volume Two of *You Might Be A Preacher If...* Your overwhelming response to Volume One has made this second laugh-a-page look at a preacher's life possible. May these pages guide you into "ever-laughing" life!

You are loved!

Stan and Mark

You've ever seen an "In Memory Of..." plate over a commode.

You've secretly wanted the head usher to give you a high-five after a particularly good sermon.

Your job description has its own three-ring binder.

You're tired of being a shepherd and would rather be a cowboy and "brand" a few in your flock.

Your Christmas bonus includes a good old-fashioned food pounding.

Running red lights in a funeral procession makes you feel important.

Everybody else has all
the answers, but you get
stuck with all the questions.

You frequently wonder, "Do I have a target on my back?"

You think atheists don't have a prayer.

•••——◉——•••

You use the word "holy" more times than Batman and Robin.

You know people who have their dispensations all right but their dispositions all wrong.

You've ever made up romantic songs to the tune of "How Great Thou Art."

Everybody stops talking when you enter the room.

You "Will preach for food."

You've discovered that people are like wheelbarrows —— they go only as far as they're pushed.

You wish Nike would make clerical clothing.

You've ever lied at a funeral.

$\cdots\!\!-\!\!\bullet\!\!\odot\!\!\bullet\!\!-\!\!\cdots$

"Family night" is ever spent in a hospital lobby.

Your wife is the church janitor.

You hate beepers and cellular phones.

You spend more time on the phone than your teenager.

The car you're driving won't jeopardize your church's nonprofit status.

You have your own ideas about the "dead in Christ."

You wish people would hurry up and unwrap their spiritual gifts.

You live in a glass house.

You're "all things to all people."

You thank the Lord everyday for Caller ID.

You always read the obituaries.

You've ever wanted to tell Brother "Know-it-all" a thing or two.

The last change you saw in church was in the offering plate.

You've thought of developing a soundproof booth for people who cough in church.

Your steering committee could use a front-end alignment.

You've ever wanted to try multilevel tithing.

You'd like to see a board member change their mind, 'cause the one they've got ain't worth keeping!

You have to leave town to get a day off.

Your office is "prayer-conditioned."

You've ever suffered an anxiety attack while playing Bible Trivial Pursuit.

You know people who have too much time on their hands and not enough on their knees.

You know how many committee members it takes to change a light bulb.

You wonder why people who have some time to kill want to spend it with you.

You've never said anything past twenty minutes that amounted to anything.

You get your second wind when you say, "And in conclusion..."

Your Daytimer is the size of a family Bible.

You've ever wanted to give somebody a piece of your mind, but knew you couldn't spare any.

You're "To Do" list is alliterated.

···➤●◉●➤···

You'd love to sleep in on Sundays.

You're on your toes when you're on your knees.

You've ever been to a "bored" meeting.

You've thought of selling "skyboxes" in a fund-raising campaign.

People know you're "laying up treasures in heaven" by looking at your car.

You've ever been compared to the former pastor.

You need a crash course on patience.

You've thought about offering Starbucks coffee to attract new attendees.

You wish Sister "Talk-a-lot" would get caught in her own "mouthtrap."

You read Lamentations on Monday mornings for devotions.

You're last in line at potluck dinners.

You buy more donuts than the police department.

You've ever felt like you were a couple of hot dogs short of a church picnic.

Your stomach gets upset when people begin their conversations with, "I hate to tell you this..."

You do the work of three men —— Larry, Curley, and Moe.

You've prayed that the Good Shepherd would lead some of your flock to greener pastures.

Your church is like a box of chocolates —— pretty on the outside with nuts on the inside.

You see "those who sleep in Him" on a weekly basis.

You've ever had to explain that
the Epistles were not
the wives of the apostles.

You've got a boat called "Visitation."

The church of your dreams has turned into a nightmare.

You've ever cut your golf score in half by playing nine holes.

The ideas you bounce off of board members really do.

The only people who like change in your church are the wet babies.

You'll preach better sermons only when John Maxwell writes better books.

Your car tires are balding faster than your head.

There are days when you couldn't even "save" a seat.

All your "pen pals" have names that are eight-digit numbers.

Anybody has ever asked you, "Will they serve deviled eggs in heaven?"

Your kids are responsible for mowing the church yard.

You'd like to talk to a few deacons about the possibilities of "home churching."

Your cat chases the church mouse.

You're partial to the Willow Creek model but your church is more like the Dead Sea.

You have an eye for fifteen-passenger vans.

People tend to think you were born again last night.

You wish someone would steal some of your sheep.

You know that cell groups are necessary for a successful prison ministry.

You are lay-driven.

You have more books about God than the local library.

You have more Bibles than the Gideons.

You'd trade all your books and Bibles for one that would show you how to get people to change.

You're one of God's life preservers.

You've ever needed a "faith-lift."

God loves you and the church board has a wonderful plan for your life.

You're like a banana — every time you leave the bunch, you get "skinned."

You drool every time you see the 500,000 people in the stands at the Indy 500.

People think you're an airport shuttle service.

You've ever been asked what it's like to work only one day a week.

You've seen more religion at a pool hall than you've seen at a church softball game.

You might be a big church pastor if... your church directory comes in three volumes.

You've anonymously telephoned your church's own dial-a-prayer line.

You can diagnose staff infection.

You enjoy holding people under water.

You wonder if faith healers get sick.

You've never played cards but you "See that hand."

You have "Saturday Night Sermons" and "Sermons in a Minute" Internet Web sites saved in your Favorites file.

You own a "parsonal" computer.

You have an open mind and a mouth to match.

You'd like to recruit some of Wal-Mart's greeters.

You've encountered a number of nodding acquaintances.

You've ever wanted to make French fries out of some of your pew potatoes.

1 Corinthians 1:21 is your life-verse.

You've ever asked for the clergy discount at a wholesale club.

You know which of these do not belong: K.J.V., R.S.V., T.L.B., C.E.V., N.A.S., F.B.I, N.K.J.V., N.I.V., G.N.B., and C.I.A.

You rise to the occasion, but don't know when to sit down.

You've ever looked into a bowl of cereal for a snap, crackle, and pop message.

Your benedictions have ever caused a "great awakening."

You're tired of people being "behind you 100 percent."

You said what you thought at board meetings, you'd be speechless.

You know Hell's Angels are not just a motorcycle gang.

You know what a vestibule is.

You could build a mansion with all the "constructive" criticism you've received.

You've ever preached a sermonette to Christianettes.

You've tried a little Miracle-Gro on your church.

You graduated from seminary and were put out to pastor.

You've ever received a phone call at 4:00 A.M. and the caller asks, "Did I wake you?"

You know why they call them "pews."

You've been encouraged to screen for the lead role in the remake of *One Flew Over the Cuckoo's Nest.*

You feel like a nonprophet organization.

You can spot a church shopper through a stained glass window.

Your sound man is tone deaf.

You've been there, preached that.

You've ever wanted to be the target of a drive-by prayer group.

Every time you see a movie you get at least five "new and inspired" sermon illustrations.

Your Bible has more side notes than printed text.

You're used to seeing the groom perspiring and the father of the bride crying.

You'd never marry a woman named Gomer.

You've got a fabulous sermon on humility.

"Annual Church Meeting" and "Armageddon" are one in the same to you.

While you talk, people wonder what they are going to eat for lunch.

People clip their fingernails while you talk.

People do anything but listen while you talk.

You've ever been called a "Holy Roller" at a bowling alley.

You've taught people everything you know and they still act stupid.

You use the pray-as-you-go plan.

You talk in other people's sleep.

Your children have biblical names.

You've ever been asked to lead in silent prayer.

You might be a Baptist preacher if you know you're going to heaven and not to Disneyland.

You're friendlier than a wet dog.

Transients know you by name.

But once again, the simplest way to know for sure that you're a preacher is when you would live your life over again and do the same things —— face the same struggles, study your brains out, and work one thousand hours a week —— all for half the pay and recognition you now get. That's when you know for sure you're a preacher.

About The Authors

Dr. Stan Toler is Senior Pastor of Trinity Church of the Nazarene, Oklahoma City, Oklahoma. For the past six years, Stan has served as Model Church Instructor for INJOY, a leadership development institute for pastors. This position enables him to travel across the United States, conducting seminars in stewardship, model church growth, missions, and leadership. Stan is also host of the television program, "Leadership Today."

Mark Toler-Hollingsworth is Senior Pastor at First Nazarene Church in Edmond, Oklahoma. Mark loves people and loves to laugh. Each Sunday his message is flavored with "heavenly humor." Mark has two daughters, Sarah and Mariah. And yes, his wife Mary plays the piano!

Other published works and manuals by Dr. Toler include:

You Might Be A Preacher If... (co-authored with Hollingsworth)
The Minister's Little Devotional Book (co-authored with H. B. London, Jr.)
Minute Motivators
Stewardship Starters
Church Operations Manual
Church Administration Forms and Letters
Minister's Little Instruction Book
ABC's of Evangelism
A Pastor's Guide to Celebrations and Events
101 Ways to Grow a Healthy Sunday School
God's Never Failed Me, But He's Sure Scared Me to Death a Few Times
All Year Church Event Book (co-authored with Elmer Towns)
The People Principle, Transforming Laypersons into Leaders

For speaking engagements contact:

Stan Toler
P.O. Box 950
Bethany, Oklahoma 73008